a Pocket Bible Study & Journal

Hayley DiMarco

D1316392

Hungry
Planet

R
Revell
a division of Baker Publishing Group
Grand Rapids, Michigan

© 2008 by Hungry Planet

Published by Revell
a division of Baker Publishing Group
P.O. Box 6287, Grand Rapids, MI 49516-6287
www.revellbooks.com

Printed in the United States of America

ISBN 978-0-8007-3224-0 (pbk.)

Creative direction: Hungry Planet
Interior design: Sarah Lowrey Brammeier

Contents

How to Use This Book   4

Week 1

To Date or Not to Date?   8

Week 2

Really Biblical Dating   17

Week 3

Purity and Temptation   37

Week 4

Honesty or TMI?   65

Week 5

Who Should You Date?   87

Week 6

Finding the One   109

How to Use

It's PB&J time. Time to feast on the hearty protein of God's Word mixed with the sweet goodness of grace. Let the truth stick to the roof of your mouth and satisfy your hunger. This study will offer a full meal on the subject of dating. In it you can expect to learn the purpose of dating, if dating or waiting is best for you, and much more about God and your dating thought life. Unlike other Bible studies, this one will help you by giving you the answers you look for when wanting to know about spending time with the opposite sex. It isn't just a fill-in-the-blank, hope-you-got-it-right kind of study. It's a guided tour of God's Word, filled with helpful

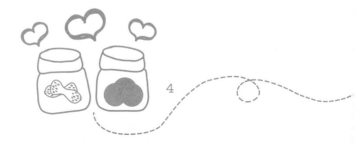

This Book

suggestions and truths as well as thought-provoking and self-examining questions.

This is a study that you can do by yourself or in a group. You can lead a group of your peers or find an adult to lead it for you. Just go online at www.hungryplanet.net and download the leader's guide of your choice, and you are off and running!

This study is for people who are ready to date, thinking about dating, or already dating. Whatever your position, I hope you will get a lot out of this study on dating and the opposite sex!

Now sit down, take a bite, and enjoy!

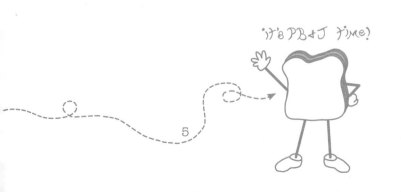

it's PB&J time!

Your Study Crew

What's up?

Make a list!
Who's in your crew?

Okay, now just some notes to get you started. First of all let me just say that I hope you are doing this book with at least one other person of the same sex. I'm sure it would be fun to do it with your significant other, but my advice is not to do that. Studying God's Word together has a way of creating intimacy, and with that feeling of intimacy comes a greater risk of temptation. When couples who aren't yet engaged do studies together, they can become so caught up in and turned on by the spirituality of it all that they lose sight of the dangers of being intimate with someone they aren't married to. And in some instances people have used the illusion of spirituality to seduce another person—using talk of spirituality for their own sexual gain. I'm not saying that your bf/gf is like that; I'm just saying, it happens. So find someone of the same sex as you to do this study with, please,

please, please! It's the best way to be honest with yourself and with God while you do the study and also to guard your heart and body at the same time.

Okay, now that I've given that speech, let me just encourage you to find at least one of your pals to do this with. Sure, you can do it on your own, but with a friend or a group of same-sex friends you'll get much more out of it. It's a great way to have accountability and share God-conversations and revelations. As you work through the questions and talk about them with each other, you'll learn much more than if you just do it alone.

Once you get your gang together and they all get their books, make plans to meet once a week to go over one chapter. Be prepared to be honest and talkative. Don't just give yes and no answers; be real, dig deep, and share. That's the best way to study and to learn. The more you can learn about God's thoughts and his plans for your life as a believer, the more healthy and happy your life will become. So call a friend or two, or three and get this study started!

Note for Group Leaders:

Don't forget to check out the leader's guides on our website. There are two. One is for an adult leading the group, and one is for you if you want to lead your friends. A guide will help you answer the hard questions and keep the gang on task. So check out www.ifuse.com and download that guide today!

To
Date
or Not to
Date?

Depending on your experiences, dating can be either the most amazing or the most devastating thing in the world.

Dating can make you feel the best you've ever felt, or it can rip your heart out. No matter what you say about dating, you can't say it's boring. Of course you can say that not dating is super boring, but that is all in how you look at it. For some dating is not even an option, either because of school, parents, or a commitment to kiss it good-bye. Maybe you have the option but you just aren't sure if or how you want to go about dating. So let's start our study with a look at the big question: to date or not to date?

Dating, Waiting, or Still Debating?

So what do you think? Is dating for you? Are you in love, in like, just crushing, or looking for "the one"? Whatever your answer to that, I'll bet that dating is in the front of your mind and a topic you just can't seem to get away from. So what are your thoughts on the subject? Are you for or against? Or just waiting to decide? I'm guessing that since you picked up this study, you'd like to get some good insight from the Bible to help you out with the topic. Duh! So let's get things started with a little introspection.

_wait!

1. What kind of info would you like to get from God's Word on the subject of dating?

2. Do you think there is a biblical way to date? If so, describe it.

3. What kinds of rules do your parents have when it comes to your dating life?

4. What about your dating history do you wish you could change?

5. Have you and your parents agreed to any dating rules or restrictions?

6. Have you broken any of those?

7. What is the purpose of dating?

8. Do you think there is just one right person out there for you?

9. What are some dating or marriage relationships that you admire and why?

You probably already have some definite ideas about dating, and that's okay. Just promise me that you'll keep an open mind when it comes to God's Word and allow it to mold your current thoughts and make them clearer and more holy. You don't have to agree with your friends when it comes to dating. And there might not even be one absolutely perfect right answer for everyone. But there are some things that you need to consider before choosing your dating plan. It's also important to talk with your parents about the subject because ultimately they set the rules for your life, at least while you live under their roof. So share with them what you're learning and find out their thoughts if you don't already know them. Dating can be a tricky subject in some households, so please just remember to honor your parents as God calls you to. And then be sure to be honest with yourself and your friends as you find out more about God's Word and its role in your life both in and out of relationships.

Were You Made for Dating?

Before we jump into studying God's Word, I want to make it clear that the Bible really doesn't include any verses on dating. Dating is a relatively new concept. The Bible *does* talk about relationships, however, both in examples and in commands. There aren't any specific commands on whether to date or to avoid it altogether or on how to date, so what you'll see here are words from God on relating to one another, managing your emotions, and being obedient. I hope you will find that all the verses you study shine some kind of light on your dating or waiting life, and I hope they will give you insight not only into dating but also into how to live and how to love others around you.

Now let's crack our Bibles open and get this study started, shall we?

Read Exodus 20:12

> "Honor your father and mother. Then you will live a long, full life in the land the Lᴏʀᴅ your God is giving you."

1. Why do people call this "the first commandment that comes with a promise"?

2. According to this verse, if you honor your parents, what do you get?

3. What does it mean to honor your parents?

4. If your parents are wrong or crazy, do you still have to honor them?

5. How do you honor nonbelieving parents?

Read 1 Corinthians 6:12 (NIV)

"'Everything is permissible for me'—but not everything is beneficial. 'Everything is permissible for me'—but I will not be mastered by anything."

1. How might this verse apply to dating?

2. What would it mean to be mastered by your dating life?

3. Are you or have you ever been mastered by your dating life?

Read Romans 14:14 (NASB)

> "I know and am convinced in the Lord Jesus that nothing is unclean in itself; but to him who thinks anything to be unclean, to him it is unclean."

1. What does Paul (the writer of this verse) mean by "unclean"?

2. If "nothing is unclean" in and of itself, what can make a thing "unclean," according to Paul?

3. How might this apply to dating or even waiting?

Read Romans 14:23

"If you do anything you believe is not right, you are sinning."

1. How does this verse describe sin?

2. Are there any things you do that you think aren't biblical or right but you do them anyway? Like what? Be specific.

3. How can something be both acceptable and sinful at the same time?

Dating is something that you are going to have to take a stance on. Either you'll choose to date, to wait, or to skip it altogether. But debating it with yourself only wastes time. When it comes to deciding what's right for you, always start with your parents. What do they want for you? Talk with them, get their ideas. If they don't have any, then you've got some decisions to make. Talk to God, **Talk to God,** decide **why** you want to date and **what** kind of person you want to date, and start to make some **godly decisions** about your life.

decide why you want to date and what kind of person you want to date, and start to make some godly decisions about your life. Because unless you have the gift of celibacy (i.e., no sex for ever and ever), you're gonna have to get married some day. That's how it works. So let's see if we can't help you get a better idea of you and your dating or waiting life.

Check, Please!

Like all good dates I hope that after reading week one you are thinking, *Let's do that again sometime.* What you read might not have been what you expected but hopefully it's shedding some light on the world of dating and you. Don't worry, there's lots more to come; we just needed to get your take on the whole affair in order before diving into the date itself. So let's talk later, or if you're ready to go, dive right into week two and we'll keep our date study going.

> "Honor your father and mother. Then you will live a long, full life in the land the LORD your God is giving you."
>
> Exodus 20:12

Week 2

Really Biblical Dating

So what is the purpose of dating?

Is it purely a way to pass time, or is there something more to it? Lots of people just date to have fun and not be lonely. But for the most part, dating does serve a purpose. The majority of people date with the intention of finding someone to marry. And those who only date for fun, well, more often than not, once they find someone they can't live without, they get married. Dating is the way you find out what you like and don't like in a relationship and ultimately who you can and can't live without. Some people call it "courting," which simply means dating with the intention of marrying. So whether they are taking dates as they come or looking for the one they will marry, ultimately most people who date want to find someone to marry. Whether you're thinking about wedding bells right now or saying, "Are you kidding me?" understanding the ultimate purpose of dating will help you better understand God's thoughts on the subject. If dating is used to meet and find the one you will marry, then studying God's thoughts on marriage and what that means and looks like will only help you to better understand the dating process and all that goes along with it.

Study Dates

First, let's look at some of the purposes of marriage:

18

$$1 + 1 = \cancel{2}\; 1$$

Read Matthew 19:4–6

> "'Haven't you read the Scriptures?' Jesus replied. 'They record that from the beginning "God made them male and female."' And he said, 'This explains why a man leaves his father and mother and is joined to his wife, and the two are united into one.' Since they are no longer two but one, let no one separate them, for God has joined them together."

1. What is Jesus referring to in the first sentence?

2. What does it mean to become "one"?

3. What does the last sentence mean?

4. What does this verse tell you about dating relationships?

5. What does it tell you about premarital sex?

Read Genesis 1:28 (NIV)

"God blessed them and said to them, 'Be fruitful and increase in number; fill the earth and subdue it. Rule over the fish of the sea and the birds of the air and over every living creature that moves on the ground.'"

1. Who is God talking to here?

2. What is he commanding them to do?

3. Based on this verse, what might you say is one purpose of marriage?

4. Why do you think God assigned this task to a married couple?

Read 1 Corinthians 7:9

> "But if they can't control themselves, they should go ahead and marry. It's better to marry than to burn with lust."

1. According to this verse, why should some people get married?

2. What does this tell you about the dating relationship?

God has specific thoughts on marriage. These are not all of them, but they give you an idea of the purpose of marriage and the importance of it. Knowing the purposes of marriage will help you as you think about who to date and how to date.

Biblical Dating Techniques

Now let's take a look at biblical dating techniques throughout the ages. Like I've said, there was no such thing as dating when the Bible was written, but there were engagements and marriages happening. So let's look at how the people of biblical times handled the bringing together of two people who would become one flesh.

Read Genesis 29:18–20

> "Since Jacob was in love with Rachel, he told her father, 'I'll work for you seven years if you'll give me Rachel, your younger daughter, as my wife.' 'Agreed!' Laban replied. 'I'd rather give her to you than to someone outside the family.' So Jacob spent the next seven years working to pay for Rachel. But his love for her was so strong that it seemed to him but a few days."

1. Why did Jacob offer to work for seven years?

2. Who made the decision on who Rachel would marry?

3. How does this compare to modern ideas of dating or courtship?

It's all for you, My love!

4. Girls, how would you feel if your dad and some random guy decided who you would marry and when?

5. Guys, how would you feel if you had to work for seven years to get a wife?

Of course, this isn't the end of this tale. You've probably heard that Rachel's dad tricked Jacob and after seven years of hard work gave him his older daughter instead. Ugh! Talk about a bait and switch. But notice that Jacob didn't take him to court and storm off—take a look at Genesis 29:21–30 to find out the rest of the story.

Read Genesis 24:34–51

> "'I am Abraham's servant,' he explained. 'And the Lord has blessed my master richly; he has become a great man. The Lord has given him flocks of sheep and herds of cattle, a fortune in silver and gold, and many servants and camels and donkeys. When Sarah, my master's wife, was very old, she gave birth to my master's son, and my master has given him everything he owns. And my master made me swear that

I would not let Isaac marry one of the local Canaanite women. Instead, I was to come to his relatives here in this far-off land, to his father's home. I was told to bring back a young woman from here to marry his son.

"""But suppose I can't find a young woman willing to come back with me?" I asked him. "You will," he told me, "for the LORD, in whose presence I have walked, will send his angel with you and will make your mission successful. Yes, you must get a wife for my son from among my relatives, from my father's family. But if you go to my relatives and they refuse to let her come, you will be free from your oath."

"'So this afternoon when I came to the spring I prayed this prayer: "O LORD, the God of my master, Abraham, if you are planning to make my mission a success, please guide me in a special way. Here I am, standing beside this spring. I will say to some young woman who comes to draw water, 'Please give me a drink of water!' And she will reply, 'Certainly! And I'll water your camels, too!' LORD, let her be the one you have selected to be the wife of my master's son."

"'Before I had finished praying these words, I saw Rebekah coming along with her water jug on her shoulder. She went down to the spring and drew water and filled the jug. So I said to her, "Please give me a drink." She

24

quickly lowered the jug from her shoulder so I could drink, and she said, "Certainly, sir, and I will water your camels, too!" And she did. When I asked her whose daughter she was, she told me, "My father is Bethuel, the son of Nahor and his wife, Milcah." So I gave her the ring and the bracelets.

"'Then I bowed my head and worshiped the LORD. I praised the LORD, the God of my master, Abraham, because he had led me along the right path to find a wife from the family of my master's relatives. So tell me—will you or won't you show true kindness to my master? When you tell me, then I'll know what my next step should be, whether to move this way or that.'

"Then Laban and Bethuel replied, 'The Lord has obviously brought you here, so what can we say? Here is Rebekah; take her and go. Yes, let her be the wife of your master's son, as the LORD has directed.'"

1. Who asked the servant to get a wife for Isaac?

2. What were the requirements for Isaac's wife?

☑ meet girl
☑ talk to parents
☑ trade camels
☐ marry girl

3. How did the servant pick a girl for Isaac?

4. Who made the decision whether or not Rebekah would marry Isaac?

5. Does this seem more like a business deal or a chick flick?

6. What does this tell you about biblical dating techniques?

From reading those verses I'm sure it's become painfully clear that in biblical days the rules of "dating" were much different than they are now. For the most part the girl's parents determined who would marry their daughter, no dating involved. The guys could make advances, but they made them in the direction of the parents or family and then often had to do all kinds of things in return for their approval. So looking through the Bible for hints of biblical dating becomes a scary concept when you see how things were done back then. But that's not all; check out the price of love.

The Price of Love

In biblical times, once a couple was hooked up by the parents, then another exchange often had to be made. A dowry, a gift of money or property given to get a girl, would be given by the guy to the girl's parents. Now, before the girls get all heated, let me just say that this wasn't like the guy was buying her or anything; it was just a sign of the monetary value of the girl to the guy. It was a way the guy could prove he was serious and that he knew she was valuable to the parents. Let's take a look at the price of biblical dating, shall we?

Read Genesis 24:53 (NIV)

> "Then the servant brought out gold and silver jewelry and articles of clothing and gave them to Rebekah; he also gave costly gifts to her brother and to her mother."

1. What did the family get in return for their daughter?

2. How does this resemble the modern dating ritual?

3. How could all these gifts be a good sign to the family?

Can I Marry her?

Read Exodus 22:16–17 (NIV)

"If a man seduces a virgin who is not pledged to be married and sleeps with her, he must pay the bride-price, and she shall be his wife. If her father absolutely refuses to give her to him, he must still pay the bride-price for virgins."

1. According to these "biblical dating rules," what must a man do if he seduces a girl?

2. Why do you think he would have to marry her?

3. Who do you think set the "bride-price"?

I'm serious!

She is valuable!

Other Reasons for Marriage

For the good of the country?

In biblical times marriage was more a fulfillment of legal and familial obligation than a case of true romance. Many alliances were formed and destroyed by who married who. Biblical dating techniques didn't require feelings of love and devotion; they merely required commitment and cooperation. Of course this seems kind of cold and creepy in our modern world of meeting and falling in love, but if you want to know what biblical dating looked like, let's peek at a few more peeps.

Week 2

The Girl's Consent

Dating in biblical times wasn't always controlled by the parents. We see instances of the girl being asked her opinion as well. Of course, she didn't get time to get to know the guy or date him, but she did get to decide if she would go home with the messenger they sent to collect her or not. For example, Genesis 24:57–58 says, "'Well,' they said, 'we'll call Rebekah and ask her what she thinks.' So they called Rebekah. 'Are you willing to go with this man?' they asked her. And she replied, 'Yes, I will go.'"

I will take care of her!

"When Boaz had finished eating and drinking and was in good spirits, he went over to lie down at the far end of the grain pile. Ruth approached quietly, uncovered his feet and lay down. In the middle of the night something startled the man, and he turned and discovered a woman lying at his feet. 'Who are you?' he asked. 'I am your servant Ruth,' she said. 'Spread the corner of your garment over me, since you are a kinsman-redeemer.' 'The LORD bless you, my daughter,' he replied. 'This kindness is greater than that which you showed earlier: You have not run after the younger men, whether rich or poor. And now, my daughter, don't be afraid. I will do for you all you ask. All my fellow townsmen know that you are a woman of noble character. Although it is true that I am near of kin, there is a kinsman-redeemer nearer than I. Stay here for the night, and in the morning if he wants to redeem, good; let him redeem. But if he is not willing, as surely as the LORD lives I will do it. Lie here until morning.'"

Kinsman-Redeemer

When an Israelite was obliged to sell his inheritance because of poverty it was the duty of the nearest relative to redeem it for him.[1]

1. Freeman, James M.; Chadwick, Harold J.: Manners & Customs of the Bible. Rev. ed. North Brunswick, NJ : Bridge-Logos Publishers, 1998, S. 202

1. What do you think a "kinsman-redeemer" was? Look it up if you don't know.

2. What did Ruth do in order to let Boaz know she needed him?

3. What does this tell you about biblical dating techniques?

Read 1 Samuel 18:20–25 (NIV)

"Now Saul's daughter Michal was in love with David, and when they told Saul about it, he was pleased. 'I will give her to him,' he thought, 'so that she may be a snare to him and so that the hand of the Philistines may be against him.' So Saul said to David, 'Now you have a second opportunity to become my son-in-law.' Then Saul ordered his attendants: 'Speak to David privately and say, "Look, the king is pleased with you, and his attendants all like you; now become his son-in-law."' They repeated these words to David. But David said, 'Do you think it is a

small matter to become the king's son-in-law? I'm only a poor man and little known.' When Saul's servants told him what David had said, Saul replied, 'Say to David, "The king wants no other price for the bride than a hundred Philistine foreskins, to take revenge on his enemies."' Saul's plan was to have David fall by the hands of the Philistines."

1. How did David and Michal get together?

2. What did David have to do for Saul in order to get her? (Before you start giggling uncontrollably, think about this request as one that basically meant "Kill all the Philistines and bring me proof.")

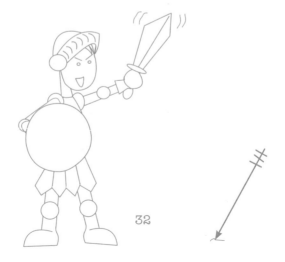

3. Girls, how does it make you feel to see the words "I will give her to him"?

4. Guys, what do you think about what Saul did to David?

5. Saul had a definite purpose for marriage. Can you think of any other uses for marriage in biblical days?

Read 1 Kings 3:1

"Solomon made an alliance with Pharaoh, the king of Egypt, and married one of his daughters."

1. Why did Solomon marry Pharaoh's daughter?

2. Who decided this marriage should take place?

Read Hosea 3:1–3 (NIV)

"The LORD said to me, 'Go, show your love to your wife again, though she is loved by another and is an adulteress. Love her as the LORD loves the Israelites, though they turn to other gods and love the sacred raisin cakes.' So I bought her for fifteen shekels of silver and about a homer and a lethek of barley. Then I told her, 'You are to live with me many days; you must not be a prostitute or be intimate with any man, and I will live with you.'"

1. What did God ask Hosea to do?

2. How did Hosea do it?

3. Hosea 3:4–5 says, "This shows that Israel will go a long time without a king or prince, and without sacrifices, sacred pillars, priests, or even idols! But afterward the people will return and devote themselves to the LORD their God and to David's descendant, their king. In the last days, they will tremble in awe of the LORD and of his goodness." Based on this, what do you think was the purpose of this marriage?

"And the elders of the assembly said, 'With the women of Benjamin destroyed, how shall we provide wives for the men who are left? The Benjamite survivors must have heirs,' they said, 'so that a tribe of Israel will not be wiped out.' . . . So they instructed the Benjamites, saying, 'Go and hide in the vineyards and watch. When the girls of Shiloh come out to join in the dancing, then rush from the vineyards and each of you seize a wife from the girls of Shiloh and go to the land of Benjamin.' . . . So that is what the Benjamites did. While the girls were dancing, each man caught one and carried her off to be his wife. Then they returned to their inheritance and rebuilt the towns and settled in them."

1. What did the Benjamites do?

2. Why did the Israelite elders let them do it?

The archaic approach

Let's Do This Again Sometime

No study of dating is complete without a thorough understanding of biblical dating techniques and reasons for marriage. Even though obviously few if any of them apply today, it is very interesting to see the ancient purposes and methods for bringing two people together. Today it's easy to get caught up in the romance of it all, but remember that God's Word doesn't command romance or even promise it. In fact, for centuries he commanded people to marry for anything but romance. That doesn't mean romance is bad; it just means you need to put your love life into perspective. Think about God's purpose for your life and the life of the one you dream about. Remember that dating isn't just for fun—it has a purpose, and that purpose is marriage. If you aren't ready for marriage, then maybe you aren't ready to date. Looking at dating from a more objective point of view will ultimately help you to see things God's way instead of the way of your passions and fantasies. Look at things from God's perspective and find freedom from stress and loneliness. I'm not suggesting we get back to these biblical dating examples, so don't freak. Just know your history and know how people did it for thousands of years before you.

Purity
and
Temptation

Okay, so we've seen relationships of old, and hopefully you've made a few decisions about your own future relationships.

Now no study on dating would be complete without touching on the touchy subject of purity. But rather than just dive into "Don't do it!" "Save yourself for marriage!" and all that stuff you've heard before, let's back it up a bit and look at your mind. What kinds of things do you think about when it comes to the opposite sex? Take this self-assessment and find out.

1. How many times a day do you think about someone of the opposite sex who you like?

2. Do you ever fantasize about someone you like?

3. Have you ever been tempted when you looked at a hot bod?

4. Do you love romantic movies and things that help you dream of the perfect love?

5. Do you look at porn?

6. Do you ever find yourself thinking about going further with your bf or gf than you already have?

You might not want to share the answers to these with anyone right now, and that's okay. But take time to answer them for yourself. Think about the state of your mind. How often is it filled with sexual thoughts? Understanding where your thoughts spend their time is super-important when it comes to creating a clean mind focused on right things and not dangerous things.

A Clean Mind

Most people probably spend more time talking about physical purity than about mental purity, but as you'll soon see , the mind is where everything gets started so no study on purity would be complete without out a journey into it. Let's take a look and see what God's Word has to say about the subject of your mind and the things you use it for.

Read Matthew 5:28

"But I say, anyone who even looks at a woman with lust in his eye has already committed adultery with her in his heart."

1. What does it mean to look at someone lustfully?

2. Look at your Bible to see who is saying this. Why do you think he says that looking is the same as doing?

3. How can you commit adultery in your heart?

4. What does this tell you about sin and your mind?

5. Can you sin without ever physically doing anything?

It all starts here!

Proverbs 23:7 (NKJV)

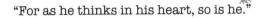

"For as he thinks in his heart, so is he."

1. What does this mean to you?

2. Based on what you think about the most, what kind of person are you?

3. Can you spend most of your time thinking evil thoughts and not be evil?

4. Can you spend most of your time thinking holy thoughts and not be holy?

5. According to this verse, how important are your thoughts?

What kinds of things cause your mind to wander onto the opposite sex and to think about things like fooling around or making out? According to God's

Word, if you think it, it's like you've already done it. So does that give you permission to go ahead and actually do it? Of course not. God knows what's going on inside your head, and if you think you can get a free pass on the "doing it" part just because you've sinned in mind already, you've made a big mistake. The thing to get out of this is that your thoughts are just as important as your actions. So check what goes into your mind so you can control what goes on in it and thus control what you do and don't do. If you want to be pure, then you have to begin with your mind. That's where it all gets its start, both good and bad.

"What I want to do I do not do, but what I hate I do."

(Romans 7:15 NIV)

If you struggle with your thoughts and desperately want to change, don't get depressed. There is hope. You aren't alone. Many others have struggled the same as you. In fact, the guy who wrote a lot of the Bible, Paul, had the same problem. Take a look at his thought process and see if it doesn't sound a lot like yours. It's important to understand the struggle you are going through. Admit it and know that you can beat it, but also know that you have someone on your side. **Read Romans 7**, and be sure to read **Romans 8:1** as a fantastic conclusion.

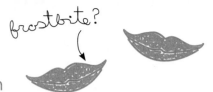

frostbite?

A Clean Mouth

The next step in search of purity takes us from your head to your mouth. What goes in your mind comes out your mouth, and that can spell disaster for a lot of us. Being sexually pure isn't just about not doing it; it's about not thinking about it and not talking about it. Sound harsh? Well, let's look at God's Word to see just how important all this really is.

Read Colossians 3:8

> "But now is the time to get rid of anger, rage, malicious behavior, slander, and dirty language."

1. Why would Paul be asking you to get rid of these things?

2. According to this verse, what things does God want you to get rid of?

3. Why would he ask you to stop with the "dirty language"?

4. What do you think a follower of Christ should consider to be "dirty language"? (Don't say it; just talk about the kinds of things you think should be off-limits.)

5. What's a good litmus test for your tongue? In other words, how can you decide what kinds of things you will avoid in the future?

Read Matthew 15:11 (NIV)

> "What goes into a man's mouth does not make him 'unclean,' but what comes out of his mouth, that is what makes him 'unclean.'"

1. Open your Bible and read the verses that come before this one: Matthew 15:1–10.

2. What exactly is Jesus talking about here?

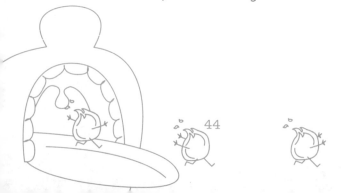

44

3. How can what comes out of your mouth make you unclean?

4. What are some examples of Christians speaking things that might make them unclean?

What goes into your head controls what comes out of your mouth. And both are majorly important. The best way to control your mouth is to control what you let in your mind and what you let your mind play with. If your mind is easily entertained by bad or sinful thoughts, then you've got to break that habit. You have to find other things to fill your mind with—godly things, holy things— to replace the bad stuff. Then you have to find ways to shut your mouth. Talking about sexual stuff is just as bad as thinking about and doing sexual stuff. So monitor your thoughts and your speech to see where you might be missing the boat when it comes to your sexual purity. Purity—it's not just about not "doing it" anymore!

But wait, there's more! So far you've seen that your thoughts and your words affect your purity. Now let's look at how your actions, even if they seem innocent to you, can affect your purity. Seems absurd and maybe a little harsh, but the truth is that even though your actions might seem totally nonsexual, you still might be playing around with sexual immorality. Want to find out how? Check it out:

Read Ephesians 5:3 (NIV)

> "But among you there must not be even a hint of sexual immorality, or of any kind of impurity, or of greed, because these are improper for God's holy people."

1. What is God forbidding in this verse?

2. Why is it forbidden?

3. What is sexual immorality? Look it up and talk about it until you understand what it means.

caution

4. What are some things that people around you do that "hint" at the fact that they are fooling around?

5. Why would God go so far as to say that even hinting about it is bad?

Read Colossians 3:5–6

"So put to death the sinful, earthly things lurking within you. Have nothing to do with sexual immorality, impurity, lust, and evil desires. Don't be greedy, for a greedy person is an idolater, worshiping the things of this world. Because of these sins, the anger of God is coming."

1. What are you called to put to death?

2. What are some ways you can put those things to death?

47

What Is Fornication?

I looked up *fornication* in Webster's dictionary, and here is what it said:

fornication: consensual sexual intercourse between two persons not married to each other

I looked up *intercourse* just to be clear about all the terms, and here is what it said:

intercourse: physical sexual contact between individuals that involves the genitalia of at least one person

How many people do you know who think that the things they are doing aren't "sex," so they aren't sinful? Most Bible translations use "sexual immorality" in place of fornication, and now when you see that, you'll know exactly what they are talking about. God prohibits it. He calls it sinful, and so what a mess to be doing it all along and not know it. It's an easy justification to make. But not anymore. Knowledge is a powerful thing. And now that you know what fornication is and that God considers it sin, it's time to understand the consequences for deciding that fornication is okay for you.

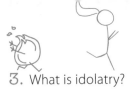

3. What is idolatry?

4. What does the final sentence mean?

Read 1 Corinthians 6:18–20

"Run away from sexual sin! No other sin so clearly affects the body as this one does. For sexual immorality is a sin against your own body. Or don't you know that your body is the temple of the Holy Spirit, who lives in you and was given to you by God? You do not belong to yourself, for God bought you with a high price. So you must honor God with your body."

1. According to this verse, what makes sexual sin worse than others?

2. What does it say that your body is?

3. How can you honor God with your body?

49

It's really important to understand the meanings of the words you read in the Bible and want to obey. If you pretend not to know the real meaning or just hope to avoid it as long as possible, you are lying to yourself. Before you go on another date make sure you know what God means when he talks about sex and sexual immorality and how far is too far.

The Punishment

This might seem like a real downer but bear with me. I think it's important to understand how seriously God takes this business of purity and sex before you're married. So just quickly look at this verse:

Read 1 Corinthians 6:9–11

"Don't you know that those who do wrong will have no share in the Kingdom of God? Don't fool yourselves. Those who indulge in sexual sin, who are idol worshipers, adulterers, male prostitutes, homosexuals, thieves, greedy people, drunkards, abusers, and swindlers—none of these will have a share in the Kingdom of God. And that is what some of you were. But you were washed, you were sanctified, you were justified in the name of the Lord Jesus Christ and by the Spirit of our God."

1. Who does this verse say will not make it to heaven?

2. What hope is there for these people?

3. If any of those describe you, what can you do today to make a change?

4. What does it mean to be justified? How does that make you feel?

Your sexual purity is more than just a Christian marketing campaign or the obsession of the adults around you; it's a command by the Creator of the universe. And when God commands something, it's always important to fully understand what he's talking about. Now that you've come this far in this study, you should have a thorough understanding of sexual immorality and purity. No more guessing or hoping that what you're doing isn't part of the sin list. Sexual purity will not only affect your spiritual life but also have a huge impact on your emotional and social life. Doing what God says is good for you in every way, even if on the face of things it looks like a huge hassle. Ultimately it will be the best thing you've ever done. Before we go on to the next chapter, spend some time thinking about the areas of your life where you've slipped up on the purity front. Think about ways that you can get back on track and help your friends to do the same. To help you out, let's do a little study on the place sin gets its start: temptation.

Temptation

If you had a chance to go back in time and kill Hitler, would you? Of course killing is a sin, but think of the greater good your one sin would accomplish. Hard to resist, huh? Temptation is similar to that dilemma—if I do something I know I shouldn't do in order to get something I really want, is that really so bad? At what point does it become bad? Is it okay in the case of stopping mass murder? What about in the case of love? Is it okay to do something wrong in order to get something oh so right? Where do you draw the line?

Temptation is always in front of you. It sits in front of you in class, on the train, and at the mall. Temptation looks good, oh so good, and it promises you so very much. So how do you know what to do when faced with temptation?

looks good ...

1. Let's start off with the basics: what is temptation? Try to put your thoughts into a definition.

2. Here's how *Nelson's New Illustrated Bible Dictionary* defines *temptation*: "an enticement or invitation to sin, with the implied promise of greater good to be derived from following the way of disobedience." With that definition in mind, make a list of some common temptations when it comes to the opposite sex:

3. What are some good ways to avoid those temptations?

Read James 1:12–15

"God blesses the people who patiently endure testing. Afterward they will receive the crown of life that God has promised to those who love him. And remember, no one who wants to do wrong should ever say, 'God is tempting me.' God is never tempted to do wrong, and he never tempts anyone else either. Temptation comes from the lure of our own evil desires. These evil desires lead to evil actions, and evil actions lead to death."

1. In the passage above, circle who God blesses. Then put a box (like a gift box) around what they will receive. Then underline all forms of the word *tempt* (tempted, temptation, etc.).

2. According to James, where does temptation come from?

3. Read the first sentence again. What is another way to think of your temptation?

Temptation comes from the lure of our own evil desires. These evil desires lead to evil actions, and evil actions lead to **death**.

4. What, according to this verse, is the outcome of temptation when it is fully acted upon?

54

It's important to understand that being tempted isn't a sin; it's what you do with that temptation that determines your sin output. Temptation *will* come, but you can pass the test and stay faithful to your God. Let's get down to the nitty-gritty of how to do it.

Kicking Temptation

Temptation comes to all of us. It's part of being human. Even Christ himself was tempted (see Matthew 4:1–11). But temptation doesn't have to be the beginning of sin; in fact, it never has to become sin at all. Still, temptation can easily lead you to do things you would never do if you had your mind about you. And that's especially true when it comes to the opposite sex. It's so easy to let your feelings and your hormones take charge of your mind, and then all bets are off. So what do you do if you are dating or even just crushing on someone and temptation hits?

1. Use the escape route.

Read 1 Corinthians 10:13

> "But remember that the temptations that come into your life are no different from what others experience. And God is faithful. He will keep the temptation from becoming so strong that you can't stand up against it. When you are tempted, he will show you a way out so that you will not give in to it."

1. What things can you learn about God from reading this verse?

2. Why should the first sentence make you feel better about your temptations?

3. What are some ways you can look for the "way out" when you are in the middle of a temptation?

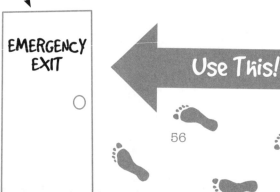

EMERGENCY EXIT

Use This!

4. In what ways could you find those "ways out" before you get in the middle of the tempting situation?

Read 2 Timothy 2:22

"Run from anything that stimulates youthful lust. Follow anything that makes you want to do right. Pursue faith and love and peace, and enjoy the companionship of those who call on the Lord with pure hearts."

1. What's the first thing this verse calls you to do?

2. What does it tell you to do in place of that thing you run from?

3. What do you think God considers a "pure heart"?

2. Avoid temptation.

Read 1 Corinthians 5:9–11 (NIV)

> "I have written you in my letter not to associate with sexually immoral people—not at all meaning the people of this world who are immoral, or the greedy and swindlers, or idolaters. In that case you would have to leave this world. But now I am writing you that you must not associate with anyone who calls himself a brother but is sexually immoral or greedy, an idolater or a slanderer, a drunkard or a swindler. With such a man do not even eat."

1. Underline all the kinds of people listed in the verse above.

2. What is good about avoiding these kinds of "believers"?

Poke Poke
Poke
Poke

58

3. What "way out of temptation" does this verse offer you?

4. How does this verse apply to who you date?

Read Proverbs 4:23 (NIV)

"Above all else, guard your heart, for it is the wellspring of life."

1. Circle the first three words in the verse above. What does that mean to you? Translate it into your own words.

2. What is a "wellspring"?

59

3. What are some practical ways to "guard your heart"?

4. What does this have to do with temptation?

3. Don't let anyone become your obsession.

Read two definitions

obsession: a persistent disturbing preoccupation with an often unreasonable idea or feeling
idolatry: immoderate attachment or devotion to something
(Merriam-Webster's Collegiate Dictionary)

1. How might either of these words be involved in a relationship or a lack of relationship?

2. Why is it dangerous to allow another person to become your obsession?

Read Romans 1:25 (NIV)

"They exchanged the truth of God for a lie, and worshiped and served created things rather than the Creator."

1. According to this verse, what or who is not to be worshiped?

2. How might this verse be applied to the dating world—either yours or that of your friends around you?

Read 2 Peter 2:19

"For you are a slave to whatever controls you."

1. What makes you a slave?

2. In what ways can a person allow himself or herself to be controlled by their bf or gf or a relationship itself?

3. Is it possible to be controlled simply by the thought of someone?

4. Why do you think God doesn't want that for you?

5. What are some ways to make sure you are not enslaved by your love life?

Read Matthew 6:24 (NIV)

> "No one can serve two masters. Either he will hate the one and love the other, or he will be devoted to the one and despise the other."

1. What are some things in a dating relationship that can master you?

2. If God is your master, how should that affect your love life (or lack thereof)?

4. Avoid the slippery slope.
Read Song of Solomon 1:2 (NIV)

> "Let him kiss me with the kisses of his mouth—
> for your love is more delightful than wine."

1. Why do you think that this passionate love is compared to wine?

2. How can physical affection affect your choices?

Temptation can put up a good fight, but if you are willing to prepare and put in the work ahead of time you're more likely to find success.

When it comes to dating and purity, temptation is always somewhere in the car. So how are you gonna handle the temptation that comes your way? Purity isn't easily maintained. The natural state of things is just the opposite. A room that isn't cleaned and kept up will quickly become an incredible mess. No work is required to create a mess; it just arrives on its own. Leave a quart of milk on the counter for a few days and its purity will quickly fade. Things left unattended effortlessly become foul and messy, and keeping things clean and pure takes work and attention. Your purity is no different. If you want to be faithful and obedient to God's Word, then you'll have to make purity a priority. But the beauty of doing things God's way is that, in the end, you will benefit enormously. The hard work will one day pay off, and your purity will be your reward and the reward of your future love. And above and beyond all this dating stuff your purity is ultimately a gift to God for a very good purpose:

> "If you keep yourself pure, you will be a utensil God can use for his purpose. Your life will be clean, and you will be ready for the Master to use you for every good work."
>
> 2 Timothy 2:21

Honesty or TMI?

TMI!

Stop talking
now!

Didn't need
to say it

A little
too honest

Honesty

Half True

White Lie

Lying

Pants
on fire!

Purity is a super-important subject to the children of God and a no-brainer when it comes to the topic of dating, but this chapter might not be so obvious.

I mean, of course you know that honesty is the best policy and nobody likes a liar and all that. You know that lying is bad . . . but what about those little white lies people tell, especially when they are trying to impress someone? Or what about the lies you tell yourself—things you think about that are in no way true but that you just can't stop pondering? Every day you have to choose whether to lie or tell the truth. And lying can destroy not only your relationship but your own peace of mind.

On the other extreme is sharing too much information. A lot of time people share too much information in an effort to bond with someone, to get them to like them, or just because they fear lying and so they just tell people everything. And that all leads to TMI. You've seen it before, someone you are with tells you every little detail of their lives. They talk and talk, on and on as if all you have to do is listen. That's what's called a boring date. So how much information you share or don't share with your date is an important thing to know.

If you lie or give TMI you could scare off your crush before you get a chance to let the love unfold. So let's take a look at how honest is too honest and how lies affect you and your relationship.

Lying to Get What You Want

When people lie just to take advantage of someone else, it's really ugly. I mean, you hear about it or it happens to you and you are shocked at how deceptive people can be. But not all liars have evil motives. Some people lie just to make things work out, or to protect someone else's feelings. Some people might even lie to help you out. And that seems pretty nice. Like if you ask them to lie to your parents for you or to lie to the person they are dating so that you can date them too. Lying is a weird thing; we hate it when it happens to us, but sometimes we make exceptions for it if we think something we want is really important. But one of the things you have to remember is that if I will do it for you, I'll do it to you. As you date you learn about people's character, and if they are willing to lie once they'll be willing to do it again. So before we dive into the Bible study part of this chapter let's do another little self-assessment.

1. Have you ever lied to make someone feel better?

Pants on Fire

2. Have you ever told someone you loved them when deep down you weren't sure if you did or not?

3. Have you ever lied to someone in order to get them to like you more? (For example, telling them you liked a band they liked even though you didn't.)

4. In your opinion, is it ever okay to lie? Explain.

5. Rate these things on a scale from bad to worse—bad being 1 and worse being 5.
   __ Stealing
   __ Lying
   __ Cheating
   __ Hating
   __ Gossiping
   Explain your ratings.

6. What are some examples of "little white lies"?

little white lies

7. Is this kind of lying bad, or is it okay because they are "white lies"?

8. Would you rather:
   (a) sometimes hide the truth in order to keep people happy or keep from hurting them?
   (b) use the truth to your advantage?
   (c) be totally transparent with everyone—no secrets?
   (d) other: _____

9. How do you feel when someone you love and/or trust lies to you?

10. How do you feel when someone you know tells you a white lie?

11. What do you think when your friend tells someone else a lie in front of you?

Big huge scary lie

12. What are some ways you think that people lie without saying anything at all?

13. Are there any lies that you like to hear (i.e., "You look great today" or "You're the best player on the team")?

God's Truth on Lying ← don't do it!

It's easier to see that lying is a bad thing when it happens to you. And when it comes to dating, lies can be even harder to bear. Many relationships are destroyed because of malicious lies or lies told just to keep someone from being hurt. No matter what side of the lying you

Socially Acceptable?

According to the book *The Day America Told the Truth*, 91 percent of Americans lie routinely. Of those, 36 percent tell dark, important lies; 86 percent lie regularly to parents; 75 percent lie to friends; 69 percent lie to spouses; 81 percent lie about feelings; 43 percent lie about income; 40 percent lie about sex.[1]

1. *USA Today*, Jan. 9, 1992, p. 4D

are on, God has something to say about changing the truth to make it work for you.

Read Leviticus 19:11

"Do not steal. Do not cheat one another. Do not lie."

1. What three things are forbidden in this verse?

2. Why do you think lying is such an important topic in the Bible?

3. Which one of these sins do you think is the worst?

4. Is lying ever okay?

5. If you were dating someone and found out they had done any of these to you, how would you feel? And what would you do?

Week 4

lies lies lies lies

Read John 8:44

"For you are the children of your father the devil, and you love to do the evil things he does. He was a murderer from the beginning. He has always hated the truth, because there is no truth in him. When he lies, it is consistent with his character; for he is a liar and the father of lies."

1. How does this verse describe the devil?

2. What does "the father of lies" mean?

3. Why would the devil be obsessed with getting people to lie?

4. What kinds of things can lying do to a relationship?

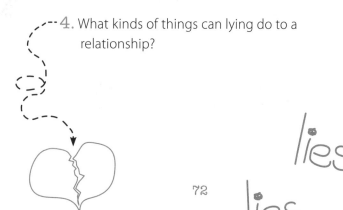

lies

lies

Read John 8:31–32

> "Jesus said to the people who believed in him, 'You are truly my disciples if you remain faithful to my teachings. And you will know the truth, and the truth will set you free.'"

1. According to this verse, what will the truth do?

2. How does that happen?

Read Proverbs 26:28 (NIV)

> "A lying tongue hates those it hurts, and a flattering mouth works ruin."

1. What does this verse say about people who lie?

2. In what way can a flattering mouth "work ruin"?

don't you
Feed Me
your lies!

3. In light of this verse, do you think that flattery is ever okay? When? Why?

4. What are some of the destructive results of lying?

5. "Sticks and stones may break my bones, but words will never hurt me." Is this saying accurate?

6. Why are some people hurt by words while others seem unfazed by them?

Read Revelation 22:15 (NIV)

> "Outside are the dogs, those who practice magic arts, the sexually immoral, the murderers, the idolaters and everyone who loves and practices falsehood."

1. What does this verse mean by "outside"?

2. Who is out there?

3. Why do you think these kinds of people are kept out?

4. What does it mean to "practice falsehoods"?

5. What's the difference between that and telling the occasional lie?

You could say that it's kinda clear that God hates liars. He hates lies and he hates the father of lies. Lying is a slippery slope. What seems like just a little white one can quickly turn into a tangled web. When it comes to honesty and lies, what is your habit? Do you find yourself slipping in a little white lie here and there just to protect yourself? What if it won't hurt anyone? Or what if it's only to yourself? If the truth sets you free, then what do you think a lie is going to do? Let's take a look at the lies you tell yourself.

Lying to Yourself

Most people accept lies when they come from themselves. Like how I used to lie to myself all the time about being in love. I told myself I would just die without it. I would think about how miserable I was and how much I wanted a guy. Ugh! Silly girl. I bought the lie that I was miserable simply because no guy loved me. And so I became miserable not because of that but because I was *telling* myself that. Make sense? It's a weird situation. You lie to yourself about stupid things like attention, popularity, clothes, looks, or anything else you obsess about, and pretty soon the lie you've held on to for dear life has made you miserable. Lying isn't okay, even when it's to yourself. And the fatalistic thoughts that can occupy your mind are lies. The truth about life for a child of God is much sweeter. So when it comes to your inner monologue, what's the theme? Is it depression and emptiness or hope and excitement? Time for a self-assessment!

1. When you have a crush, is he or she all you can think about?

death by lack of boyfriend

2. When you're not in a relationship, what do you think about more: the things you're missing out on by not having a significant other or the freedom and opportunities you have by being unattached?

3. How much time do you spend thinking about ways to get them to go out with you?

4. When you are in a relationship, do you usually think it will last forever?

5. When a relationship ends, do you usually think it is your fault? How much time do you spend looking back at the past or what went wrong?

6. Do you worry a lot or let things slide off your back?

like water off a Duck

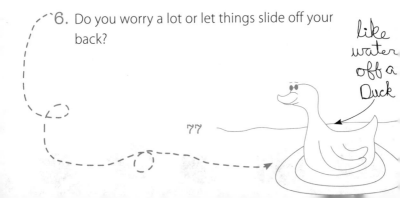

7. Do you concentrate on the negative or the positive?

8. Do people often tell you, "You're overreacting" or "Stop reading so much into it"? If yes, think about those times and see if you can find any lies you might have been telling yourself.

The things you think about most will tell you if you are being honest with yourself or believing a bunch of lies. Let's look at a couple verses for more insight on your mind.

Read Philippians 4:8–9 (NIV)

> "Whatever is true, whatever is noble, whatever is right, whatever is pure, whatever is lovely, whatever is admirable—if anything is excellent or praiseworthy—think about such things. . . . And the God of peace will be with you."

1. What does God tell you to think about in this verse?

2. What kinds of thoughts would be excluded from this list?

3. How well do you practice this way of thinking?

4. What are some ways you could change your mind to think these kinds of thoughts?

5. Make a list of things you can think about with regard to your dating life that would be true, right, pure, etc.

6. According to this verse, what happens to people who think good, true thoughts?

7. What does a mind focused on the God of peace look like?

Change Your Mind

1. Find the lies. Before you can tell yourself the truth, you'll first have to find all the lies that you are buying. Spend some time this week looking for the places you might be lying to yourself. The best way to find those is to start with the trouble in your life. What things bug you or stress you out? What places in your life need improvement? Once you can identify those areas, you can start to pay attention to how you think about those things. What kinds of thoughts do you allow yourself to think about them? Make a list of some of the things you find yourself repeating that are inconsistent with faith. Things like "This will never get better," or "My life is miserable," or feelings of fear, worry, or resentment. There are too many areas of lies to list them all right here, but I encourage you to really take some time to find all your lie spots. You have to identify your negative tendencies before you can replace them with faithful ones. So make a list of the lies you tell yourself. Start with the ones in "Lying to Yourself" and see if you can't find more.

2. Just say no! Once you've found your lies, decide to always say no to them. Whenever you think a lie, say "No!" or imagine one of those loud game show buzzers you hear when a contestant gets an answer wrong. Then change your thoughts to something true.

3. Make a truth list. For those really stubborn lies you can't seem to shake, you can make a list of truths to fight them. God's Word is called a sword for a reason. Write down some verses that help you stop the lies, and keep those verses with you at all times. Read your list when you start feeling bad or being dishonest with yourself. This will help you kick the bad habit of lying to yourself.

8. According to this verse, what are some reasons that peace might not be yours right now?

You might be the most honest person in the world, except when it comes to yourself. Lying to yourself by thinking the worst, concentrating on your pain and misery, is the opposite of honesty. It's an outright lie, and God finds lying appalling. Don't miss this: lies you allow yourself to believe are lies through and through. But they *can* be stopped. All you have to do is practice Philippians 4:8. In order to help you do that, check out the "Change Your Mind" exercise on the previous pages.

TMI

The opposite extreme of lying is TMI—too much information. Have you ever listened to someone telling you way too much? It can be agonizing, not to mention embarrassing. TMI should be outlawed, don'tcha think? But why are so many people willing to fill you in on so much oh-so-unnecessary information? I think a lot of it has to do with honesty. Sometimes we confuse honesty with TMI, thinking that in order to be honest we have to talk and talk and talk, just to make sure we cover it

And then there was this one time...
This thing with my mom...
once I was on this other date...
oh, this one guy...

all, especially when you first start dating. But that isn't true. You don't have to tell everyone everything in order to be honest, or to be real. Not only is TMI unhealthy but it's unattractive too, a total turnoff. Most people like a little mystery. We are all kind of excited by the chase and the wonder of a new dating relationship. When you give TMI too soon, you can freak the other person out and lose the mystery. Honesty is never an excuse for flooding someone with too much of your stuff. That's actually more selfish than honest. You just want to be heard and you aren't really thinking about the other person. So let's see what God has to say about the subject of TMI and see how that could apply to your next date

And then...
You wouldn't believe...

Read Ecclesiastes 10:12–14 (NIV)

"Words from a wise man's mouth are gracious, but a fool is consumed by his own lips. At the beginning his words are folly; at the end they are wicked madness—and the fool multiplies words."

It was so totally...

1. According to this verse, what is the difference between a wise man and a fool?

I got this weird thing with my toe...
I was drooling everywhere...

And my brother threw up...
My poor kitty...

2. Why do you think God cautions against talking too much?

3. How can a person be consumed by their own lips?

 Read Ecclesiastes 5:2–3 (NIV)

"Do not be quick with your mouth, do not be hasty in your heart to utter anything before God. God is in heaven and you are on earth, so let your words be few. As a dream comes when there are many cares, so the speech of a fool when there are many words."

1. What do you think is the benefit of being slow with your mouth?

2. What does the second sentence mean?

3. Put the last sentence into your own words.

Read Proverbs 15:28 (NIV)

"The heart of the righteous weighs its answers, but the mouth of the wicked gushes evil."

1. What does it mean to weigh your answers?

2. How long do you think that might take?

3. What are some examples of "gushing evil"?

Read Proverbs 21:23 (NIV)

"He who guards his mouth and his tongue keeps himself from calamity."

1. What kind of "calamity" could happen to you if you don't guard your mouth on a date?

2. What are some ways that you can guard what you say when you're on a date?

Putting the Pieces Together

In every relationship you will ever have, communication will be key, and it's very important to the health of you and your significant other to learn honesty and the art of not sharing too much. In the short run, both lying and giving TMI can feel like the best thing for the situation, but eventually both of them will catch up with you. So make sure that you practice the kind of communication that reflects who you are as a believer and that will help you to have the healthiest relationship possible. Remember, it's not about what you can get for the moment but about what each moment means for eternity. May this verse be your prayer:

"Keep me from lying to myself; give me the privilege of knowing your instructions."

Psalm 119:29

Week 5

Who Should You Date?

Okay, so we've looked at biblical relationships, purity, temptation, and honesty; and hopefully you've learned some stuff to help you out on your next date.

But without another person of interest to actually date all this learning was in vain. So the next big question that needs answering is who should you date? Is the one you are dating right now the right one for you, or is someone better out there? Will the person you are crushing on make you happy or mess up your life? Figuring out who to date can be a really hard thing to do, and even harder still is finding that one in the crowd. Luckily there are some rules of thumb that you can follow as a believer—some things you can look for in others in order to decide if they are good date material or not.

Rate 'Em to Date 'Em

Before we get into figuring out who's right for you, let's answer some Qs.

1. Name the top 5 things you look for in a bf or gf.

2. On a scale of 1 to 10, how important are the following in a person you want to date:

faith	1 2 3 4 5 6 7 8 9 10
family	1 2 3 4 5 6 7 8 9 10
grades	1 2 3 4 5 6 7 8 9 10
looks	1 2 3 4 5 6 7 8 9 10
money	1 2 3 4 5 6 7 8 9 10
body	1 2 3 4 5 6 7 8 9 10
personality	1 2 3 4 5 6 7 8 9 10
sense of humor	1 2 3 4 5 6 7 8 9 10
car	1 2 3 4 5 6 7 8 9 10
confidence	1 2 3 4 5 6 7 8 9 10
kindness	1 2 3 4 5 6 7 8 9 10

3. What characteristics do you dislike in a bf or gf? (Examples: lying, B.O., bad hair, anger, materialistic, etc.)

4. Have you ever dated someone your parents and/or friends didn't like? Why didn't they like them?

Week 5

When it comes to who you want to date, you probably have a long list of things you love and things you can't stand. And it's important to know what you like and don't like so you can ultimately find the one who's just right for you. But moderation is always key. It's important that your list is not so particular that no one could possibly fit it. Remember, no one is perfect, not one person, and waiting for perfection means you'll be waiting a long time. That said, it's still important to have some guidelines in mind before picking who you will date. So here goes.

Deal Breakers

As a believer, you shouldn't compromise on a few deal breakers when it comes to who you date. These are things that are commanded and can't be avoided. If you overlook them for a hottie who is "almost" good enough, you'll have misery on your hands in the near future. Trust me, and trust God's Word.

Deal Breaker #1: Nonbelievers
Read 2 Corinthians 6:14–16

> "Don't team up with those who are unbelievers. How can goodness be a partner with

wickedness? How can light live with dark-
ness? What harmony can there be between
Christ and the devil? How can a believer be
a partner with an unbeliever? And what
union can there be between God's temple
and idols?"

1. <u>Underline</u> the word *unbelievers* in the verse
   above. Now ⟨circle⟩ the words used to describe
   said unbeliever. Then put a <u>triangle</u> around
   each word used to describe God's people.

2. What are some ways that a believer might try
   to "team up" with an unbeliever?

3. Is dating a nonbeliever "teaming up" with
   them?

4. Is marriage to a nonbeliever allowed,
   according to this verse?

5. Why do you think God made this command?

... or heartbreak hotel ?

6. What are some practical problems you could imagine between a believer and a nonbeliever who are dating?

If you are dating a nonbeliever, stop! Not only are you forbidden from it but you are in for a world of hurt if you should end up with them forever. They will never understand you and your relationship with Christ. They won't encourage it, they will be jealous of it, and you will end up having to choose between them. It is not your job to lead them to Christ, so don't use that as an excuse. That's just using a lie in order to break God's law. Don't go there!

Deal Breaker #2: Bad Boys, Naughty Girls, and Other Bad Believers

Read 2 Timothy 3:1–5

"You should also know this, Timothy, that in the last days there will be very difficult times. For people will love only themselves and their money. They will be boastful and proud, scoffing at God, disobedient to their parents, and ungrateful. They will consider nothing sacred. They will be unloving and unforgiving; they will slander others and have no self-control.

They will be cruel and have no interest in what is good. They will betray their friends, be reckless, be puffed up with pride, and love pleasure rather than God. They will act as if they are religious, but they will reject the power that could make them godly. You must stay away from people like that."

1. Who *not* to date? <u>Underline</u> all the descriptions of what sinful (non-dateable) people do, according to this verse.

2. Do you know any people doing any of those things?

3. What does the verse say you should do with them?

4. How could this apply to who you want to date?

clear them out of your dating life!

Read 1 Corinthians 5:11

> "You are not to associate with anyone who claims to be a believer yet indulges in sexual sin, or is greedy, or worships idols, or is abusive, or is a drunkard, or cheats people. Don't even eat with such people."

1. Underline the sins listed in this verse.

2. According to this verse, can you date a sexually active person if they are saved and forgiven?

3. What other kinds of people does this verse tell you not to date?

4. What are some idols that people you know worship? (It can be anything they are obsessed with—video games, money, clothes, popularity, drugs.)

Deal Breaker #3: Angry People

Read Proverbs 22:24–25

> "Don't befriend angry people or associate with hot-tempered people, or you will learn to be like them and endanger your soul."

1. Underline the people this verse tells you to stay away from.

2. According to this verse, what's the danger to you of having a bf or gf who gets angry easily?

Deal Breaker #4: Haters

Read 1 John 4:20–21

> "If someone says, 'I love God,' but hates a Christian brother or sister, that person is a liar; for if we don't love people we can see, how can we love God, whom we cannot see? And he has given us this command: Those who love God must also love their Christian brothers and sisters."

1. Underline "hates a Christian brother or sister" in the verse above. Is this verse about believers or nonbelievers?

2. Can you be mean to your brothers and sisters and still be a loving person?

3. What is the danger of dating someone who is mean to other people?

4. What does it say about you if you are dating a mean person?

So there you have four major categories of deal breakers—people you absolutely should not be dating. Go back now and look at all the things you underlined in all four sections and compare them to your crush. Any deal breakers there that you didn't think about till now? If so, then something has to happen. The deal has to be broken. It's up to you, though. Are you going to choose God or your crush? I know it's hard to walk away from someone you like just because they have one problem on this list. Believe me, I know—I've done it and I hated it. But I did it. And even though I cried over it, I know it was the best thing to do. Are you ready to start bringing your dating life into line with God's Word? Now's your chance.

Green Flags

Hopefully the deal breakers look like deal breakers to you and aren't that hard to accept. They should be seen as flapping red flags that tell you to slow down or turn around altogether. But there are also some green flags you can look for—signs that this person might just be a good one for you. When you are dating or want to date someone, it's important to not only avoid the bad characteristics but also look for the good ones. And it should be no surprise that God's Word talks about those green flags. As you look at the following passages, realize that when it comes to dating, you get what you give. And by that I mean that if you have these good character traits, then it's a lot easier for you to find someone with them. So as you read on, also check out yourself and see how you stack up. If you want the best, then you'll have to be the best yourself.

pretend these are green

Read Galatians 5:22–23

"But the Holy Spirit produces this kind of fruit in our lives: love, joy, peace, patience, kindness, goodness, faithfulness, gentleness, and self-control. There is no law against these things."

1. Circle all nine "fruits." Which of these come easiest to you?

2. Which are the hardest?

3. In order to move beyond your weaknesses, it's important to not spend a lot of time with someone who has your same weaknesses. In what areas do you and your crush both fall short?

4. No one is perfect, but it's important to look for someone who is interested in growing in all these areas. In what ways do you think you could spend time increasing the fruit of the Spirit in your life?

Read Colossians 3:12

> "Since God chose you to be the holy people he loves, you must clothe yourselves with tenderhearted mercy, kindness, humility, gentleness, and patience."

1. <u>Underline</u> the five things this verse tells us need to be a part of our character.

2. What does *mercy* mean?

3. Have you seen your crush act with mercy?

4. How have you shown mercy in the past year?

5. Do you know any humble people? If so, what are they like?

6. Is your crush truly humble?

Week 5

7. What are some things a person might do that would tell you that they are not practicing gentleness?

8. How might the character trait of patience apply to your dating life?

Humility Defined

Here are a couple good definitions of humility:

1. "a socially acknowledged claim to neutrality in the competition of life" (*Harper's Bible Dictionary*), and

2. "an ungrudging and unhypocritical acknowledgment of absolute dependence upon God" (*Tyndale Bible Dictionary*).

Knowing the definition of humility, look at the list below and cross out all the character traits that aren't humble:

pride   hope   selfishness   anger
arrogance   faith   love   envy   meanness
kindness   forgiveness   jealousy   gossip
backstabbing

9. Is there anything on this list that you don't think is that important in a bf or gf? If so, why not?

10. Are there any qualities in this list that you need to work on?

Read Matthew 16:24–25 (NIV)

> "Then Jesus said to his disciples, 'If anyone would come after me, he must deny himself and take up his cross and follow me. For whoever wants to save his life will lose it, but whoever loses his life for me will find it.'"

1. In the verse above, underline "deny himself."

2. Why would you, as a believer, look for someone who is practicing denying themselves?

3. In what ways have you denied yourself?

4. What are some things people do that show that they have definitely not died to self?

5. Is your crush serving themselves or God?

Read Ephesians 6:1–3

> "Children, obey your parents because you belong to the Lord, for this is the right thing to do. 'Honor your father and mother.' This is the first commandment with a promise: If you honor your father and mother, 'things will go well for you, and you will have a long life on the earth.'"

1. Underline what God is telling you to do here.

2. According to this verse, what are two reasons to obey your parents?

3. How does this apply if you don't agree with your parents?

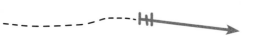

4. Why would God want you to date someone who obeys their parents?

Read Proverbs 25:28

" A person without self-control is as defense-less as a city with broken-down walls."

1. Underline "self-control" in the verse above.

2. What happens when a person has no self-control?

3. In the old days, what purpose did the city walls serve?

4. Does the person you want to date have self-control?

5. What kinds of things can you look for in the life of a person who shows they don't have self-control?

Week 5

Read Proverbs 15:22 (NIV)

"Plans fail for lack of counsel, but with many advisers they succeed."

1. What is God telling you to do here?

2. Hate failure? God has an answer. According to this verse, what can help you avoid failure?

3. How would this apply to your dating life?

4. List a few people you trust to give you godly advice.

5. Does your crush like to rush into things or get advice first? What does that say about him or her?

Read Proverbs 22:1 (NIV)

"A good name is more desirable than great riches; to be esteemed is better than silver or gold."

1. Underline the thing that this verse describes as desirable.

2. What does this verse say about a good reputation?

3. Does the person you want to date have a bad rep?

4. If you have a bad reputation, how important do you think it is to work toward making it better?

Positive Date Traits

Look back at all the positive character traits you've underlined in the previous passages and write them on the lines below:

_____

_____

_____

_____

_____

_____

_____

_____

_____

_____

_____

_____

_____

_____

From now on, when thinking about who you are dating or hope to date, look at this list and ask yourself how they measure up in each category. Think about how they act, what you've heard and seen in their lives, and ask yourself how close they are to having all of these characteristics.

God has definitely made it clear which qualities make a godly person. And there is a reason for all of them. They aren't there just to make your life a challenge; they will ultimately make your life easier, especially when it comes to who you hang with. When you see these characteristics in a person you want to date, then that is a green flag to keep looking into the possibilities. But don't rush into anything. Get to know the green flags, the dangers, and the good qualities you and your crush should be working on before you dive in too far.

If you want a relationship that works, find someone who is hungry to be more godly. Look for someone who shows some evidence of moving in that direction. And avoid the ones who are way off the mark. You aren't their savior, and thinking that it's your job to fix or save them will only bring you heartache. The most important thing of all is that you don't do this dating thing alone. Get good advice. Find out what others think of the person. Ask people you trust to give you godly advice on whether or not you are even ready to start dating. And be sure to always listen to the advice of your parents— it's the one command that gives you a promise.

> If you want a **relationship that works**, find someone who is **hungry to be more godly**. Look for someone who shows some **evidence** of moving in that **direction**. And **avoid** the ones who are way off the mark.

Putting the Pieces Together

I hope that as you've read all these verses you've applied them to your life as well as your crush's life. When it comes to who you date, think about yourself like a car. What kind of car are you? A '66 Bug, an '07 Honda, a '98 Porsche? Then look at the person you are interested in. What kind of car are they? If they aren't anywhere near the same style as you, then they might not be for you. I mean, you don't want to trade your nice new Lexus for an old beater van. Be discerning. Look for people who are good for you and trying to the same degree you are to become godly. And if you find someone who is far outperforming you in the area of faith, then get your life in order. Practice God's Word and become the kind of person they might be interested in. But in everything remember that God should be your goal before the love of your crush. The most successful dater is the one who looks to God for what they need. So remember to:

> "Delight yourself in the LORD and he will give you the desires of your heart."
>
> Psalm 37:4 NIV

Finding
the one

The main purpose of dating is to figure out if that person is the one for you—i.e., for you to marry.

Dating is a pretty new concept, not a biblical one, so figuring out how to date faithfully is a challenge. It's up to you and your parents to listen to God, to know his Word, and to decide what works best for you and your future honey. One of the biggest dangers of dating is getting physical. For generations people have experienced the dangerous side of love: the unwanted pregnancies, the broken hearts, the STDs. It's a tricky road to walk without falling into some kind of mess. But even though dating can be dangerous to your body, soul, and heart, it's still something that most people are going to do. And there's nothing wrong with that. But if you are going to date, then you've got to get the lay of the land and make some decisions in advance in order to keep yourself safe and happy.

I think every unmarried person I know is looking for love. You hope and you pray that the next one will be "the one." And that can be where a lot of the trauma comes in, because more often than not, the next one isn't "the one," and so you're bound for heartache. But

Wassup?

there are ways to guard your heart and keep an open mind to the idea that one day you will find love, all the while staying true to who God calls you to be. Before we finish this study, let's have a look at God's will for your life and see if we can't find out where "the one" for you is hiding.

God's Word Is His Will

As believers we should always be looking for God's will. You wanna be on the same page as him, obey him, and make the right choices. But it's hard, so you beg and you plead with him to tell you what to do and when to do it. And when you don't get a clear answer you can freak. It's normal, happens to all of us who really want to please God. But there is one way to find out his will that is much clearer than waiting for a sign, and that is reading his Word. God's will is summarized in the Bible. Everything we need to know about making decisions and living life is in the good book. And relying on it can take away a lot of the pressure you might be putting on yourself when it comes to finding the one.

111

Read 2 Timothy 3:16–17

"All Scripture is inspired by God and is useful to teach us what is true and to make us realize what is wrong in our lives. It corrects us when we are wrong and teaches us to do what is right. God uses it to prepare and equip his people to do every good work."

1. What does it mean for Scripture to be "inspired by God"?

2. According to this verse, what is the purpose of Scripture?

3. How can Scripture prepare you for dating?

4. How could you use Scripture to help you know if someone you like is the one?

Read Psalm 19:7–8 (NIV)

"The law of the LORD is perfect, reviving the soul. The statutes of the LORD are trustworthy, making wise the simple. The precepts of the LORD are right, giving joy to the heart. The commands of the LORD are radiant, giving light to the eyes."

1. Underline the subject of each of the four sentences above. What are all those subjects referring to?

2. Circle all the descriptions that apply to Scripture.

3. According to this verse, how might you figure out if the person you are dating is "the one"?

4. What do you think it means to "give light to the eyes"?

5. What do all of these say about the Bible and how much you can trust it to help you live your life?

Read Deuteronomy 4:2

"Do not add to or subtract from these commands I am giving you. Just obey the commands of the LORD your God that I am giving you."

1. What are you commanded *not* to do in this verse?

2. What are some ways that people disobey this verse?

3. Is there any place in Scripture where God tells you exactly who to date or marry?

4. What do you think about people who say "God told me I was going to marry you"?

5. What are some reasons that God might want you to choose who to marry?

Read 1 Thessalonians 2:13

"Therefore, we never stop thanking God that when you received his message from us, you didn't think of our words as mere human ideas. You accepted what we said as the very word of God—which, of course, it is. And this word continues to work in you who believe."

1. According to this verse, where did the words in the Bible come from?

2. What does "to work in you who believe" mean?

3. How can God's Word help you in the world of dating?

4. Write down five verses that you think can help you make good choices in your dating life.

1.

2.

3.

4.

5.

God says that in Scripture he has given you all you need to know about him and about the choices in your 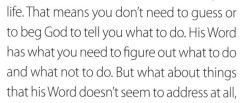 life. That means you don't need to guess or to beg God to tell you what to do. His Word has what you need to figure out what to do and what not to do. But what about things that his Word doesn't seem to address at all, like whether you should date this one or that one? How do you make those kinds of choices and still stay inside God's will?

Choosing the Right One

When it comes to things that aren't specifically in God's Word, like whether you should date or not or even who you should date, it's important to "run it by him" to determine whether what you're doing is a godly choice or a stupid one.

Read Acts 17:11 (NIV)

"Now the Bereans were of more noble character than the Thessalonians, for they received
the message with great eagerness and exam-
ined the Scriptures every day to see if what
Paul said was true."

1. What was different about the Bereans?

2. What do you think made them so noble?

3. What is Paul known for?

4. What did the Bereans do after they heard Paul
   talk?

5. What does this tell you about the things you
   read, hear, or think? What should you do
   before you believe or decide something?

week 6

After you've run everything through the filter of God's Word, the next step is all you, baby. When you've seen that the things or people you are choosing between aren't unbiblical or sinful, well, then you're good to go. See what I mean:

Read Romans 8:28

> **"And we know that God causes everything to work together for the good of those who love God and are called according to his purpose for them."**

1. According to this verse, what does God do?

2. Who does he do it for?

3. How is it possible that he can make everything work out?

4. According to this verse, what happens if you choose between two good things, like person A and person B?

A or B?

5. With this in mind, do you think that people can ever make the wrong choice in who to marry?

6. God hates divorce (see Matthew 19:6). How can Romans 8:28 be applied to marriage in order to stop people from choosing divorce?

When I was trying to make the big decision of where to move—Hawaii or Nashville—I was torn. One was a terrific ministry opportunity, and one was a great job opportunity. I really wanted Nashville but felt like God surely wanted me to choose the opportunity in Hawaii 'cuz after all, it was pure ministry. So I went to a trusted pastor and asked his help. He said, "Hayley, God lets you make the choice you want to make when you are choosing between two good things. It's like this: God has given you a playground to play on, and he doesn't care if you play on the swing set or the slide. He just wants you to stay on the playground. The choice between two good things is up to you. Do what you want." What a relief that was. And boy was he right—the desire of my heart was Nashville, so that's where I went, and that's why you are reading this book today. It all led up to this. Thank God someone helped me to stop fearing and to start moving. It was the best thing I ever did! And you can

119

use the same kind of process in finding the one. Rather than be scared and torn ("Is this the one? Am I making a mistake?"), obey God's Word, make sure "the one" is obeying too, and then make your choice. When choosing between two godly things, you can't go wrong. And always, always remember God works everything out for the good of those who love him. So ultimately no matter who you pick, if you marry them, then they *are* the one. Once you make the commitment, God is behind the choice no matter what and will work everything together for good. So stay in the Word, spend time with God, and set yourself up for making a good choice.

God Will Get You Where He Wants You

Think that it's impossible to get your life on the right track? Fear that you've messed up too much or that you'll just never get anywhere near where God wants you? If you are paralyzed and not sure what to do, don't worry. Relax. God will get you where he wants you if you are willing to be both active and patient. Check it out:

> When choosing between **two godly things, you can't go wrong.** And always, always remember **God works everything out for the good of those who love him.**

Read Acts 16:6–7 (NIV)

"Paul and his companions traveled throughout the region of Phrygia and Galatia, having
been kept by the Holy Spirit from preaching
the word in the province of Asia. When they
came to the border of Mysia, they tried to
enter Bithynia, but the Spirit of Jesus would
not allow them to."

1. What were Paul and his companions trying to
   do and why?

2. Who stopped them?

3. Was their goal a sinful one?

4. Who ultimately chose where they would go?

 ←da hand

Read Isaiah 14:27

> "The Lord of Heaven's Armies has spoken—
> who can change his plans? When his hand is
> raised, who can stop him?"

1. According to this verse, who is in charge?

2. If God has plans for your life, is there any way to change them?

3. How can he be in charge when you have free will? (Deep question!)

Even though you might not feel like it, God is always in on your life. He's in control but not bossy. He's watching over you and helping you with your choices. When it comes to dating, it can be really hard to decide what to do. But you have to keep your eyes on God and his Word and never fear that when choosing between two good things you might choose wrong. Dating is filled with all kinds of tough choices, but if you are obedient, you don't have to fear. It's only when you disobey God and go out on your own that you're going to be in trouble.

122

Get G-Rated

When it comes to dating, I can tell you one thing for sure about your dating life: God's will for you is your purity, and you've got to be on board with him on that in order to keep your heart, your body, and your soul safe and happy. Don't date without knowing that about God and without some kind of plan to help you guard yourself and the one you're dating. When it comes to your hormones, you're bound to run into the fight of your life, unless of course you've been given the gift of celibacy. But that aside, you're going to need some help. That's why you should be doing this study with at least one other person, hopefully more. Whatever the case, now is the time to put your knowledge into practice. Get together with a few of your gang and make some plans to help each other keep the purity while still having a life and not locking yourself away in a convent or monastery (not that there's anything wrong with that). Dating can be a dangerous thing or a good thing—it all depends how you choose to approach it.

Here's one way to think about it: If your life were a movie, what would your rating be? Could your little sister or your granny come to the movie of your life, or would it be way out of their league? As a believer your life should be safe for all viewers. Your goal should be to get G-rated. Not that you're going to become some kind of cartoon or Disney movie, but the explicit language, nudity, sex, and violent scenes should be deleted. My challenge to you is to make the agreement today to go G. Here's a couple tips to help you out.

Our Gang

Use the group you've been doing this study with to create a safety net. Help each other out when it comes to the dating scene. Come up with a list of questions that you are going to ask each other each week about your dating life—things like what did you do this week, who did you do it with, where did you go, and what did you do that you shouldn't have? When you know you have to fess up to someone about what you did, it's a lot easier to resist the bad stuff. So write up your own list of Qs or get online at www.ifuse.com and see what others are doing. Then agree to keep asking each other the questions on a weekly basis, especially if any one of you is dating a lot. When it comes to your dating life, you aren't an island. Enlist the help of your friends and family in order to keep the faith—in other words to not mess up and go against all the things that God has said and that you believe.

What's Your Sign?

Another way to get G-rated is to get yourself a secret sign. That's something like a ring, bracelet, or necklace that will remind you when you look at it of the commitment you've made to God to keep things clean. A ring is really good 'cuz every time you look down at where your hand is going, you can see it and be reminded of your commitment. It works wonders.

Read Deuteronomy 6:6–9

"And you must commit yourselves wholeheartedly to these commands I am giving you today. Repeat them again and again to your children. Talk about them when you are at home and when you are on the road, when you are going to bed and when you are getting up. Tie them to your hands and wear them on your forehead as reminders. Write them on the doorposts of your house and on your gates."

1. What does this verse say the Israelites should do with God's Word?

2. Why would God have them go to such lengths?

3. How could you apply this concept to yourself and the things you want to remember and practice?

There was a reason God told his people in the Old Testament to bind his Word to their foreheads. It was so they wouldn't forget it and get distracted by life. Dating can be a great experience or it can be a disaster. Just keep it G. Carry a reminder of that commitment, and get your gang all set to look after one another and help each other remember God's Word. Living a life of faith is always a challenge, and in the game of love it's especially tough. But I know you can do it if you're willing to do the work before you date.